The Christmas Gift: A Mia and Co. Adventure
Copyright © 2021 Mary Alice Archer

Published by Deep Waters Books, P.O. Box 692301, Orlando, FL 32869 | www.deepwatersbooks.com

All rights reserved. No portion of this book may be reproduced, stored in a retrieval system, or transmitted in any form by any means—electronic, mechanical, photocopy, recording, or any other—except for brief quotations in printed reviews, without permission of the author.

Illustrations and Design: Mary Alice Archer

First Printing 2021 | Printed in the United States of America

Scriptures taken from the Holy Bible, New International Version®, NIV®. Copyright © 1973, 1978, 1984, 2011 by Biblica, Inc.™ Used by permission of Zondervan. All rights reserved worldwide. www.zondervan.com The "NIV" and "New International Version" are trademarks registered in the United States Patent and Trademark Office by Biblica, Inc.™

Identifiers: ISBN: 978-1-7327480-6-4 (Hardcover) | ISBN: 978-1-7327480-7-1 (Paperback)
Library of Congress Control Number: 2021922073

Publisher's Cataloging-in-Publication data
Names: Archer, Mary Alice, author.
Title: The Christmas gift : a Mia and co. adventure / written and illustrated by Mary Alice Archer.
Description: Orlando, FL: Deep Waters Books, 2021. | Summary: Mia and her foster brothers and sisters put on a Christmas play about the greatest gift of all time: Jesus.
Identifiers: LCCN: 2021922073 | ISBN: 978-1-7327480-6-4 (hardcover) | 978-1-7327480-7-1 (paperback)
Subjects: LCSH Christmas plays--Juvenile fiction. | Christmas--Juvenile fiction. | Jesus Christ--Juvenile fiction. | Foster children--Juvenile fiction. | BISAC JUVENILE FICTION / Holidays & Celebrations / Christmas & Advent | JUVENILE FICTION / Religious / Christian / Holidays & Celebrations | JUVENILE FICTION / Family / Orphans & Foster Homes |
Classification: LCC PZ7.1.A7275 Chr 2021 | DDC [E]--dc23

This book is dedicated to my siblings—
Judy, Pat, and Mike.

And to my marvelous and creative grandchildren
— Ethan, Austin
Zephaniah, Isaiah,
Azaliah, and Hezekiah.

A BIG thank you to my loving,
patient, and supportive husband—
John.

I am thankful beyond words for Kim,
Patricia, and Seth.

The Christmas Gift

A Mia and Co. Adventure

Written and Illustrated by
Mary Alice Archer

Just then CeCe arrived carrying a big box containing two action figures, a large roll of duct tape, some gold chocolate coins, a mirror, and a handful of pennies.

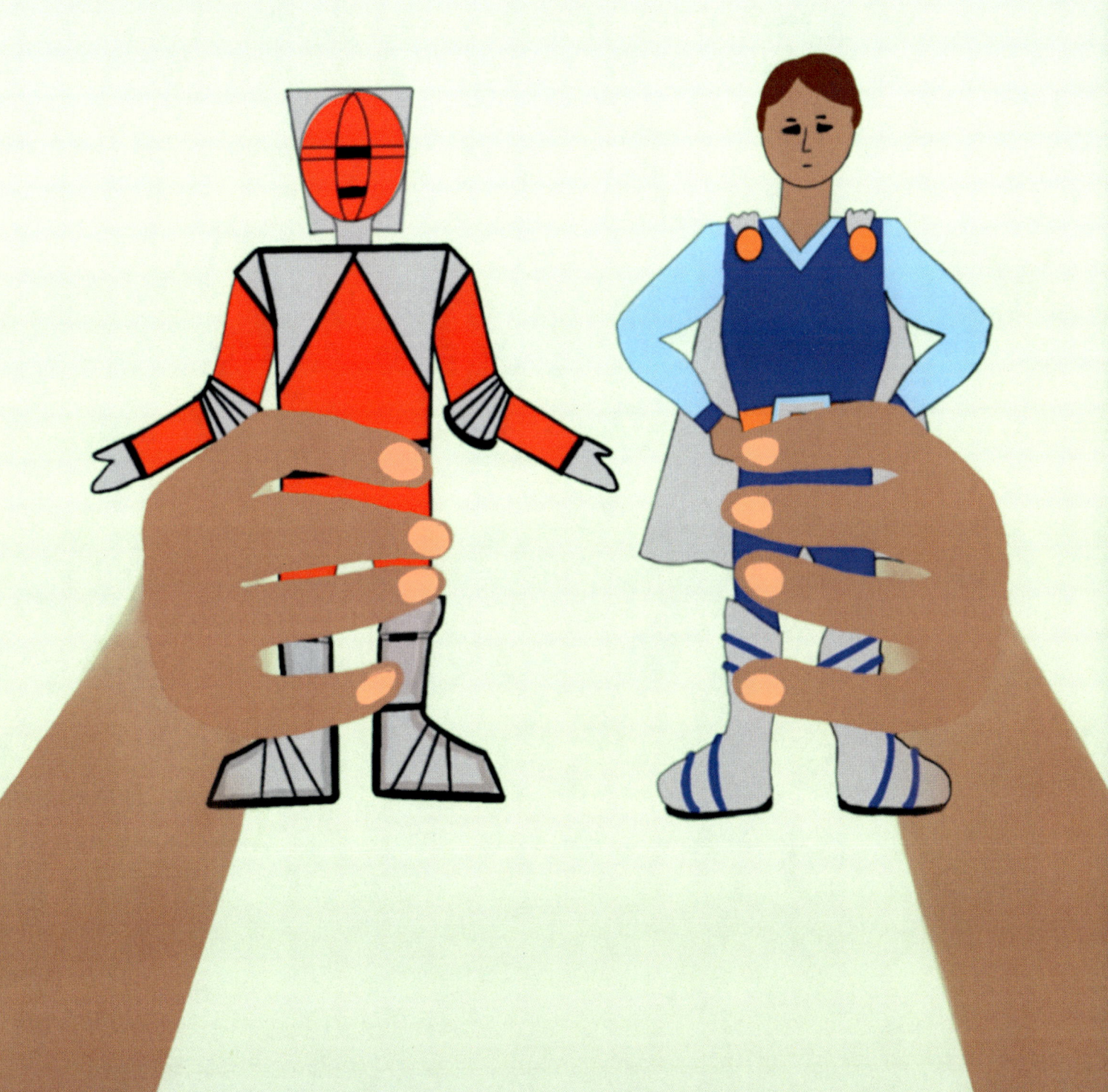

"What are you doing?" Mia asked.
"You know we are practicing for the Christmas Story tonight, don't you?"

"Yeah, and I want to be the three wise men," replied CeCe.

"Our teacher said there could have been more than three wise men," Luis stated. "The Bible never says how many wise men there were."

"Well, that's just WRONG! I've seen pictures of them," Mia declared. There's three all right."

"Whatever." Luis shrugged.

"Hot dogs? What do you need hot dogs for?" Luis frowned.

"For the franks and cents, silly." CeCe smiled. "I've already got the pennies...and chocolate gold coins, and a mirror...I'm not sure why the Wise Men brought a mirror for Baby Jesus.

Wait! That's four gifts! Maybe there were FOUR Wise Men?"

Luis sighed. "Since we don't have REAL gold, frankincense, or myrrh, those might do..."

Mia scratched her head. "How should we do shepherds and sheep?"

"I know! I'm already three people, so I'll be the shepherds, too. We can tape all my stuffed animals to Grady, and he can be the flock of sheep."

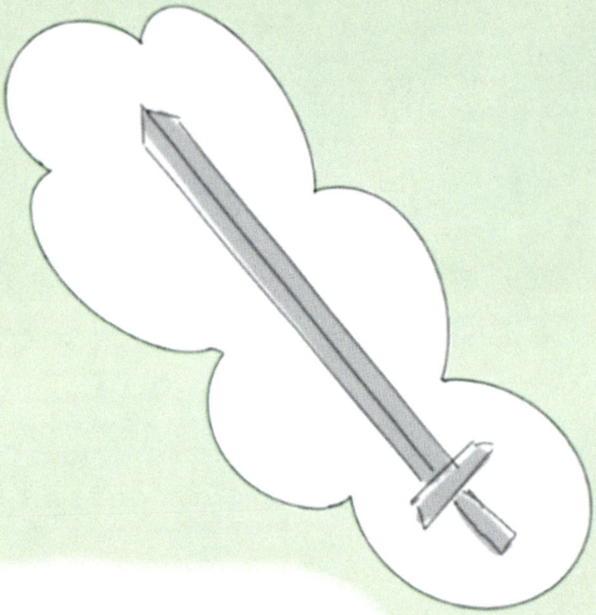

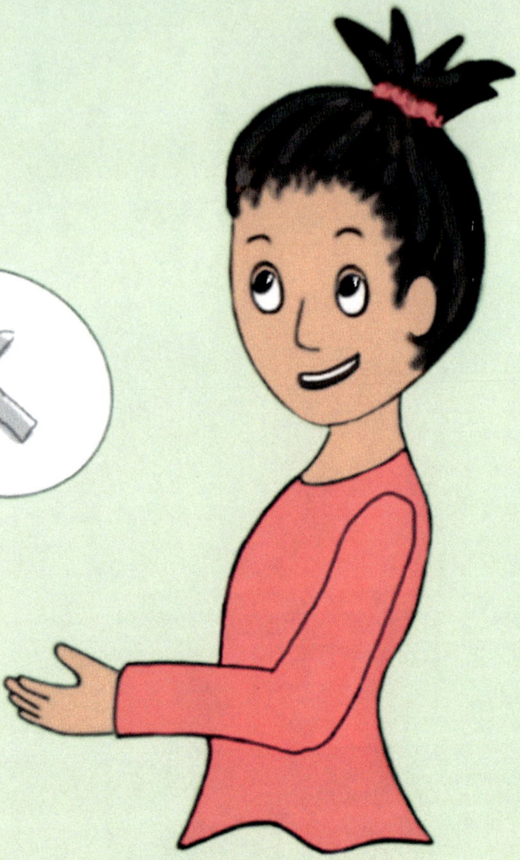

Mia sighed and rolled her eyes.
"Angels carry swords, Luis."

"That's even better! Then I'll really look like a warrior angel!" Luis responded.

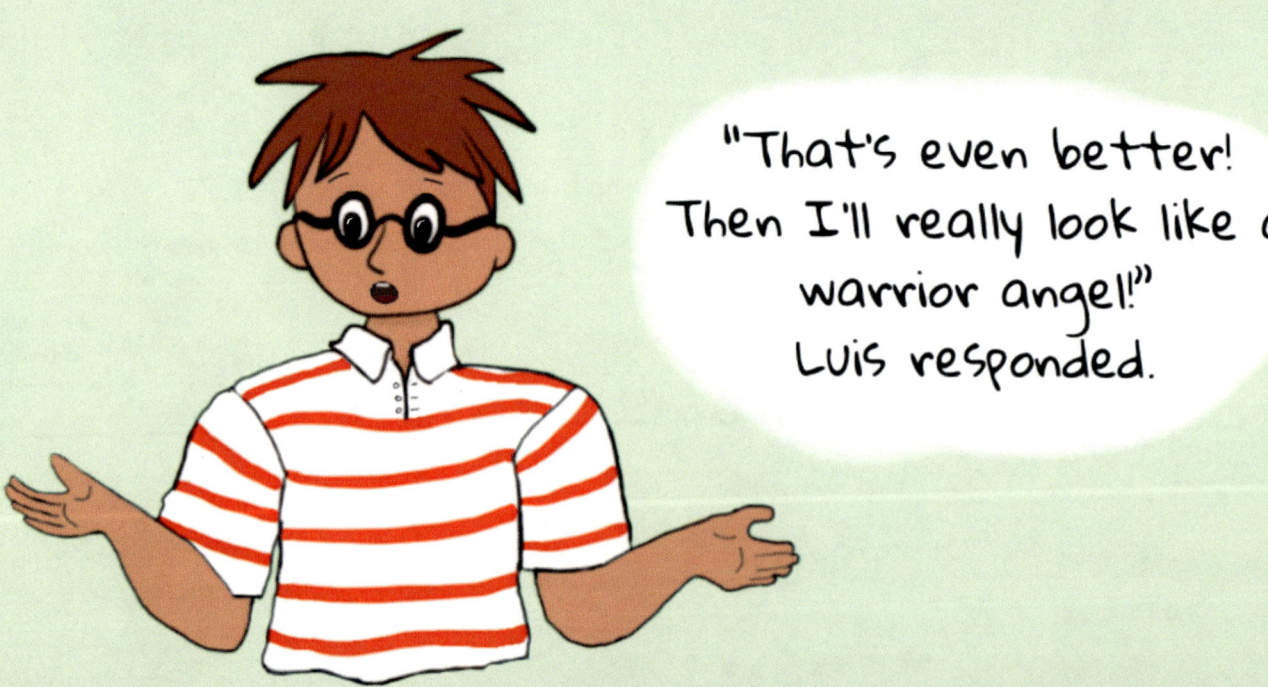

"We can use my dolly for Baby Jesus," CeCe offered. "He doesn't have any hair. Do you think Jesus had any hair when he was born?"

"Absolutely," responded Luis with a nod.

Luis squinted his eyes. "Yeah, but my teacher says Jesus was probably born in a cave where they kept sheep."

Mia laughed. "Oh, Luis! That's the silliest thing I've ever heard! Where would the other animals fit?"

"I think the most important thing is that we remember Jesus was born SOMEWHERE to be our Savior," Grady said solemnly.

Mia clapped her hands with excitement. "Okay! So let's round up all our toy animals for the flock."

"We're on it!"

"For God so loved the world, that He gave His one and only Son, that anyone who believes in Him will not die, but will have everlasting life."

"JESUS IS THE BEST CHRISTMAS GIFT EVER!"

Every good and perfect gift is from above, coming down from the Father of the heavenly lights,
who does not change like shifting shadows.

(James 1:17)

GOOD NEWS!

Have you ever...
Said something bad?
Done something bad?
Thought something bad?

The Bible tells us that these things are sin and they keep us apart from God. Did you know EVERY person in the world has sinned? THE GOOD NEWS is that Jesus came to rescue us by taking our punishment for sin by dying on a wooden cross and coming back to life.

It was Jesus's gift to us.

Now we can be part of God's family if we accept his Son Jesus's gift. How can we receive it? It's so easy. Just talk to God—he hears everything anyway—and say:

"Jesus, I believe you are God and that you died for my sins. Please forgive me, take all my sins away, and come into my heart and life."

Thank you, Jesus!
Amen!

Let's Talk About It

Here are some thought provoking questions and conversation starters to sit and ask your little ones after reading *The Christmas Gift* together.

1. Do angels have nunchucks or swords?

Several places in the Bible tell us that many angels have fiery or flaming swords—no nunchucks are mentioned. Check out Genesis 3:24; Revelation 2:12.

2. Was Jesus born in a wooden stable or a stone cave?

There are a lot of theories about where Jesus was born. Some theologians believe Jesus was born in a stone cave that was used to keep animals in during the time of Jesus's birth, and others believe Jesus might have been in the lower level of a home (like a basement) that held animals. None of them think Jesus was born in a wooden stable or a modern-day barn. They all agree that Mary swaddled Jesus and laid him down in a feeding trough or manger as the Bible states in Luke 2:7.

3. Did Mary ride on a donkey from Nazareth to Bethlehem?

The Bible doesn't say in Luke 2:5 if Mary rode in a cart, sat on a donkey, or walked the entire seventy-five miles from Nazareth to Bethlehem to be counted in the Roman census.

Find Out

We all have traditional ideas about the birth of Jesus. Are they founded on information in the Bible or the historical culture of the time? Ask an adult to help you scan the QR code below to research the following questions:

1. Were the wisemen present at Jesus's birth?

2. Did the wisemen ride camels?

3. Was Jesus born on December 25th?

What we do know is that Jesus was born into the world to save us from our sins.
And that's the best Christmas Gift EVER!

HOORAY!

Foster Families

In this story, Mia, Luis, CeCe, and Grady are all part of a foster family. Foster families are a great way to show the love of Jesus to children in need of a safe home. The National Foster Parent Association explains that foster care is:

* a chance to make the world a better place one child at a time

* one of the most challenging experiences you will have in your life

* the single most rewarding thing you will ever do

Foster families are an example of what Jesus meant when he said, "Let the little children come to me" (Matt. 19:14).

To the devoted foster families,

"Thank you for all you do! We are grateful for you."

About the Author

    Mary Alice Archer has written and illustrated an award winning children's book, *If a Cat*. She and her husband love creating YouTube videos with their grandchildren called "Bo Bo Fun!" with puppets, songs, stories, and read-alongs.

    A Southern California girl for the first forty years of her life, Mary Alice—in a moment of brilliance—moved to Central Florida where she has enjoyed teaching middle school students for over twenty-five years.

    She and her husband have three children, six grandchildren, two dogs, a Bourke's parakeet, and a Hermann's tortoise named—of course—Melville.

Made in the USA
Monee, IL
18 January 2024

52007346R00031